BEAUTIFUL South Africa

BEAUTIFUL South Africa

Johannesburg is South Africa's largest city and the industrial and financial hub of a country that is emerging, painfully but with bright promise, from the darkness of the apartheid era. This is a nation of some 40 million people and of bewildering human diversity, the contrasts vividly evident in the mix of race and language, creed, colour, culture and economic status. Variety is there, too, in the physical nature of the land: in its widely differing climates, its regions of high mountain peaks and broad grassland plains, its rugged coasts and the semi-arid flatlands of the great interior, its game-rich bushveld and the lovely hills and valleys of the south, each of the many parts displaying its own, highly distinctive character.

Johannesburg, wo Industrie und Wirtschaft pulsieren, ist die größte Stadt des Landes, das sich allmählich vom dunklen Joch der Apartheid-Ära befreit und voller Hoffnung in die Zukunft schaut. Die Mannigfaltigkeit seiner 40 Millionen Menschen, drückt sich in Rasse, Sprache, Glauben, Kultur und gesellschaftlichem Rang aus. Auch in der Natur zeigt sich ein überwältigender Kontrast: weitgehende Klimaveränderungen, Berg- und Steppenlandschaften, zerklüftete und wilde Küsten, das dürre und weite binnenländische Flachland, das tierreiche Buschveld, die reizvollen Berge und Täler im Süden–jede Region trägt ihre eigenen, unverkennlichen Merkmale zur Schau.

Première ville d'Afrique du Sud, dont elle est le centre financier et industriel, Johannesburg émerge non sans difficulté de la sombre période de l'Apartheid, mais c'est avec optimisme qu'elle s'avance vers l'avenir. Avec près de 40 million d'habitants, le pays est d'une extrême diversité. Diversité humaine d'abord, car c'est une véritable mosaïque de races, de langues, de religions et de cultures. Diversité géographique et climatique ensuite comme en témoignent ses différentes régions où l'on passe de la haute montagne à la savane, d'une côte déchiquetée aux immensités semi-désertiques du vaste plateau intérieur, de la brousse avec ses grands fauves à un paysage harmonieux de collines et vallées au sud; chacune de ces régions ayant un caractère intrinsèque.

Johannesburg was built on gold, discovered in 1886 when an itinerant Australian prospector stumbled on the Witwatersrand reef, the world's most prolific repository of the metal. The mines still enrich South Africa, though their importance has declined in recent years. Above: *A demonstration of gold-pouring.* Right: *African mine dancers.*

Johannesburg ist auf Gold gebaut. Ein umherziehender, australischer Schürfer entdeckte 1886 zufällig die größte goldführende Ader der Welt. Die Goldgruben bereichern auch heute noch das Land, obwohl in vermindertem Maß. Oben: *Das Gießen von Gold.* Rechts: *Schwarze Bergbautänzer.*

Johannesburg fut construite sur l'or. En 1886, un prospecteur australien découvrit, pratiquement par hasard, le filon du Witwatersrand, le plus prolifique du monde. Bien que son importance ait déclinée ces dernières années, la production minière est toujours un atout économique important pour le pays. Ci-dessus: *La coulée de l'or en lingots.* A droite: *La danse des mineurs.*

Gold Reef City is an imaginative reconstruction of pioneer Johannesburg, built on the Crown Mines site 6 km from the city centre. Right: *An excursion by steam train.* Below: *Street entertainment.*

Gold Reef City, 6 km vom Stadtzentrum und auf dem Gelände der stillgelegten Crown Mines errichtet, stellt Johannesburg in seinen Pioniertagen dar. Rechts: *Ein Ausflug per Eisenbahn.* Unten: *Unterhaltung auf der Straße.*

Reconstruit sur l'emplacement de Crown Mines à 6 km du centre ville, le village minier de Gold Reef City est une reconstitution authentique de Johannesburg au temps des pionniers. A droite: *Une promenade en train en vapeur.* Ci-dessous: *L'animation dans la rue.*

Pretoria, 60 km to the north of Johannesburg, is a handsome city, famed for its feathery, lilac-coloured jacaranda trees which put on a resplendent display in spring (opposite, below), *and its stately edifices, among them the Union Buildings* (below). *The statue is of Louis Botha, first prime minister of the Union of South Africa. Tradition of a wholly different kind can be seen in this Ndebele village* (opposite, above) *near Middelburg, some distance to the east of Pretoria.*

Pretoria, 60 km nördlich von Johannesburg, ist eine elegante Stadt, bekannt für ihre lilafarbenen, fiedrigen Jakarandabäume (gegenüber, unten), *und stattlichen Häuser, wie das Union Building* (unten) *Gebäude. Die Statue zeigt den ersten Premierminister der Union von Südafrika, Louis Botha. Nicht weit von Pretoria, nahe bei Middelburg, kann Tradition ganz anderer Art in diesem Ndebele-Dorf* (gegenüber, oben) *bewundert werden.*

Située à 60 km au nord de Johannesburg, Pretoria est une ville agréable, célèbre pour ses jacarandas aux douces teintes mauves (ci-contre, ci-dessous) *qui bordent ses avenues et pour ses imposants édifices.* Ci-dessous: *L'ensemble architectural des Union Buildings avec la statue de Louis Botha, le premier ministre de l'Union d'Afrique du Sud. Ce village Ndebele* (ci-contre, ci-dessus), *situé près de Middleburg à l'est de Pretoria, reflète un genre de tradition bien différent.*

A two-hour drive from Pretoria will bring you to Sun City, one of the world's largest and most lavish resort complexes. Among its features are beautifully landscaped grounds, lively gaming rooms, nightclubs and theatres (below), *and four splendid hotels, including the pyramidal Cascades* (right).

Nach zweistündiger Autofahrt erreicht man Sun City, den großartigen, fast verschwenderisch gebauten Erholungsort. Herrlich angelegte Gärten locken, aufregende Spielsalons, Nachtklubs, Theater (unten) *und vier ausgezeichnete Hotels, wie das pyramidengleiche Cascade Hotel* (rechts).

A deux heures de Pretoria, le vaste ensemble de Sun City est l'un des complexes les plus fastueux et les plus grandioses au monde. Un parc admirablement dessiné, des salles de jeu animées, des nightclubs et des théâtres (ci-dessous) *ainsi que quatre hôtels splendides–avec le fameux hôtel en forme de pyramide, le Cascades Hotel* (à droite)*–constituent quelques-unes des nombreuses attractions de Sun City.*

Sun City's newest and most glamorous component is the Lost City, whose centrepiece is the Palace Hotel (left), *an ornately elaborate place of towers and minarets, pools and waterfalls. It has 350 luxurious rooms and an entrance hall three storeys high; in the grounds are a 3 500-tree instant 'jungle' and a swimming pool with artificially created surfing waves.* Above: *A glittering array of 'slots'.*

Lost City–die Verlorene Stadt im Sun City Komplex und erst kürzlich gebaut, zieht alle Besucher in seinen Bann. Das reich verzierte Palace Hotel (links) *mit seinem 350 luxuriösen Zimmern und dreistöckigem Foyer, seinen Türmen, Minaretten, Bädern und Wasserfallen, bildet den Mittelpunkt. Dschungelartig wirkt der Garten mit seinen 3 500 Bäumen, und auf künstlichen Wellen kann man im Schwimm-bad wellenreiten.* Oben: *Ein glitzerndes Aufgebot an Münzeinwürfen.*

Lost City, la plus récente et la plus extravagante des créations de Sun City, s'ordonne autour de l'hôtel le Palace (à gauche), *ensemble très élaboré de tours et de minarets ornés de fioritures, avec bassins et cascades. C'est un hôtel de 350 chambres de luxe avec une grande entrée, situé au coeur d'une 'jungle' de 3 500 arbres et doté d'une piscine aux vagues artificielles.* Ci-dessus: *Une panoplie de 'machines à sous' rutilantes.*

For sheer scenic beauty, few parts of the country can compare with the Mpumalanga Drakensberg, a region of high peaks and forested slopes, deep green valleys, perennial streams and sparkling waterfalls. Opposite, bottom: *The Elands River falls in the southern foothills.* Right: *The intriguing fantasia of water and eroded rock known as Bourke's Luck Potholes.*

Nur wenige Gegenden können mit der beneidenswerten Schönheit der Drakensberge in Mpumalanga wetteifern. Hochaufragende Berge, bewaldete Hänge, weite, grüne Täler, perennierende Bäche und schimmernde Wasserfälle sind ihr Merkmal. Gegenüber, unten: *Der Elandsfluß Wasserfall im südlichen Vorgebirge.* Rechts: *Die faszinierende Traumwelt von Wasser und abgetragenem Fels, bekannt als Bourke's Luck Potholes ('Bourkes Glücksbringerlöcher').*

La région du Drakensberg, au Mpumalanga, offre des panoramas uniques, parmi les plus grandioses du pays que caractérisent de hautes montagnes aux versants couverts de forêts, de riches vallées verdoyantes, des torrents et des cascades. En face, ci-dessous: *Les chutes de Elands River, dans le sud.* A droite: *Les étranges marmites de Bourke's Luck Potholes, creusées par l'érosion.*

Among the high escarpment's most enchanting venues is Pilgrim's Rest, once a thriving little gold-mining centre and now a 'living museum'. The village has been preserved in its charming entirety; the houses and miners' cottages, the shop, bank and hotel are just as they were in the period 1880 to 1915. Left: *The main (and only) street.* Opposite, above: *The trading store.*

Pilgrim's Rest zählt zu den bezauberndsten Stätten auf den steilen Abhängen–einst ein emsiges, kleines Goldbergwerkszentrum, heute ein lebendes Museum, in dem der Reiz vergangener Zeiten weiterlebt. Häuser und Heime der Bergarbeiter, der Laden, die Bank, das Hotel–sie sind so erhalten wie sie zwischen 1880 und 1915 das Dorf belebten. Links: *Die Hauptstraße (und einzige Straße).* Gegenüber, oben: *Der Laden.*

Pilgrim's Rest est l'un des endroits les plus charmants de cette région. Jadis florissant village minier, c'est de nos jours un 'village-musée', extrêmement bien restauré. Son unique rue (à gauche), *bordée d'anciennes maisons, d'une banque, d'un hôtel et d'un magasin, est restée telle qu'elle était entre 1880 et 1915.* Ci-contre, ci-dessus: *L'épicerie-quincaillerie locale.*

Above: *The Blyde River Canyon, a majestic red-sandstone gorge overlooked by the massive buttresses of Mariepskop and The Three Rondavels. Among the look-out points along the area's scenic Panorama Route is God's Window* (left), *from which there are breathtaking views across the Lowveld plain to Mozambique.*

Oben: *Die imponierende Blyde River Schlucht, überragt von den mächtigen Felswänden des Mariepskop und Three Rondavels. God's Window–das Fenster Gottes–*(links) *ist einer der vielen Aussichtspunkte auf der landschaftlich herrlichen Panorama Route. Von hier genießt man einen atemberaubenden Blick über das Lowveld bis nach Mozambique.*

Ci-dessus: *Le canyon de la Blyde River, gorge de grès rouge magnifique que dominent les énormes contreforts de Mariepskop et les Trois Rondavels. La Fenêtre de Dieu* (à gauche) *offre un point de vue à vous couper le souffle: un panorama allant des plaines du Lowveld jusqu'au Mozambique s'ouvre devant vous.*

Below: *The Blyde River has been dammed at the gorge to create a lovely lake, a serene and reflective expanse of water that is home to hippo and crocodile.* Right: *The Mount Sheba Hotel, an elegant cluster of thatched buildings set in its own enchanting, and ecologically priceless, forest reserve.*

Unten: *Durch die Eindämmung des Blyde River ist in der Schlucht ein friedlicher und beschaulicher See entstanden, in dem sich Flußpferde und Krokodile wie zuhause fühlen.* Rechts: *Das Mount Sheba Hotel, strohbedeckte Gebäude in einem bezaubernden und ökologisch wertvollen Waldschutzgebiet.*

Ci-dessous: *La gorge de la Blyde River a été aménagée et on y a créé un lac splendide aux eaux sereines où vivent des hippopotames et des crocodiles.* A droite: *L'hôtel de Mount Sheba, ensemble harmonieux de maisons à toit de chaume, situé au coeur d'une charmante réserve forestière, lieu privilégié d'un point de vue écologique.*

The Kruger National Park occupies nearly 20 000 km² of Lowveld bush country to the east of the northern Drakensberg, and is haven to more varieties of wildlife than any other game sanctuary in Africa. Among its 148 mammal species are lion (below), *warthog* (right) *and the lordly giraffe* (opposite).

Von den nördlichen Ausläufern der Drakensberge, dehnt sich der 20 000 km² große Krügerpark in östlicher Richtung über das buschige Lowveld. In keinem anderen Wildpark Afrikas gibt es eine größere Vielfalt an Tieren: zu seinen 148 Säugetierarten zählen der Löwe (unten), *das Warzenschwein* (rechts) *und die hochnäsige Giraffe* (gegenüber).

Le parc Kruger s'étend sur presque 20 000 km² de brousse dans le Lowveld, à l'est du Drakensberg du nord. C'est un véritable paradis de vie sauvage et c'est le parc d'Afrique qui offre la plus grande variété d'animaux. Parmi ses 148 espèces de mammifères, on trouve le lion (ci-dessous), *le phacochère* (à droite) *et l'altière girafe* (ci-contre).

Above: *Graceful cheetah, fastest of land mammals, slake their thirst at one of the Kruger's waterholes.* Opposite, below: *A lone Burchell's zebra, of which there are more than 30 000 in the Kruger Park.* Opposite, above: *Hikers pause to examine elephant spoor on the three-day Nyalaland wilderness trail, one of several foot-safaris that traverse the park.*

Oben: *Graziöse Geparden, eins der schnellsten Tiere, löschen ihren Durst.* Gegenüber, unten: *Eins der über 30 000 Burchell-Zebras im Wildpark.* Gegenüber, oben: *Teilnehmer der dreitägigen Nyalaland Wilderness Trail Fußwanderung prüfen Elefantenspuren. Mehrere Safariwanderwege durchkreuzen den Wildpark.*

Ci-dessus: *De gracieux guépards, le plus rapide des mammifères, étanchent leur soif à l'un des points d'eau du parc.* Ci-contre, ci-dessous: *Un zèbre de Burchell, l'un des 30 000 du parc.* Ci-contre, ci-dessus: *Des randonneurs s'arrêtent pour examiner les empreintes d'un éléphant. Ils font la 'Nyalaland wilderness trail', randonnée-safari de trois jours.*

Below: *One of the Kruger's trail camps. Outside the park's western boundary are three of the world's largest privately owned reserves and some of its finest game lodges–exclusive and supremely comfortable camps staffed by rangers who are deeply versed in the ways of the wild.* Right: *Rhino in the Ingwelela reserve.*

Unten: *Eins der Lager im Krügerpark. Jenseits seiner westlichen Grenze erstrecken sich drei der größten Privat-Naturschutzgebiete der Welt, mit hervorragender, außergewöhnlich komfortabler Unterkunft und erfahrenen, mit der Natur vertrauten, Jagdaufsehern.* Rechts: *Nashorn im Ingwelela Wildpark.*

Ci-dessous: *L'un des camps de randonnée dans le Kruger. En bordure de la frontière occidentale du parc, il y a trois réserves privées, parmi les plus grandes du monde, et il y a aussi plusieurs 'lodges' haut de gamme, aux camps luxueux et au personnel très au fait en matière de vie sauvage.* A droite: *Des rhinocéros dans la réserve d'Ingwelela.*

Above: *Visitors to the internationally renowned MalaMala reserve view lion on their morning drive. The area boasts Africa's largest concentration of big game.* Left: *The Londolozi reserve's attractively cosy Bush Camp.*

Oben: *Besucher im weltbekannten MalaMala Wildpark beobachten Löwen während der morgendlichen Ausfahrt. Das Gebiet rühmt sich der höchsten Anzahl von Großwild in Afrika.* Links: *Bush Camp, die reizvolle, gemütliche Unterkunft im Londolozi Wildpark.*

Ci-dessus: *Des visiteurs en sortie matinale observant des lions à MalaMala, réserve la plus célèbre et la mieux connue internationalement. Cette région s'enorgueillit d'avoir la plus forte concentration de gros gibier en Afrique.* A gauche: *L'agréable Bush Camp situé dans la réserve de Londolozi.*

The spectacular heights of the main Drakensberg range fall almost sheer a full 2 000 m down to the green and pleasant uplands of KwaZulu-Natal, their foothills a mecca for the trout fisherman (right, above), *the hiker* (right, centre) *and the horse rider* (below). *The Tugela River* (opposite) *is among several watercourses that rise on the flat-topped massif known as The Amphitheatre, seen in the background.*

Sensationell stürzen die steilen Felswände fast über 2 000 m jäh in die Tiefe herab, in das grüne und liebliche Hochland von KwaZulu-Natal. Das Vorgebirge ist ein wahres Paradies für den Forellenangler (oben, rechts), *den Wanderer* (mitte rechts) *und den Reiter* (unten). *Der Tugelafluß, wie viele andere, nimmt seinen Anfang hochoben auf dem flachen Gipfelplateau des Amphitheaters, im Hintergrund sichtbar.*

Les sommets de la chaîne du Drakensberg ont des précipices vertigineux qui s'ouvrent sur les vertes plaines du KwaZulu-Natal quelque 2 000 m plus bas. Au pied des collines, c'est un véritable paradis pour le pêcheur de truite (ci-dessus à droite), *le randonneur* (au centre à droite) *et le cavalier* (ci-dessous). *La Tugela River* (en face) *est l'un des nombreux cours d'eau qui traversent l'Amphithéâtre, ce massif au sommet plat à l'arrière-plan sur la photo.*

Above: *Paddling pools at South Beach.* Right: *A decorative rickshaw and its Zulu 'driver', among the few that still ply the seafront.* Opposite, above: *City-centre flower market; a great many of Durban's citizens are of Indian origin.* Opposite, below: *The small-craft harbour.*

Oben: *Planschbecken in South Beach.* Rechts: *Nur noch wenige Rikschas, wie diese schön geschmückte mit ihrem Zulu 'Lenker', fahren auf der Strandpromenade.* Gegenüber, oben: *Blumenpracht im Stadtzentrum; viele Einwohner von Durban stammen ursprünglich aus Indien.* Gegenüber, unten: *Der Hafen für kleine Boote.*

Ci-dessus: *Des bassins à South Beach.* A droite: *Un 'conducteur' zoulou avec son pousse-pousse décoré, parmi les derniers qu'on trouve encore sur le front de mer.* Ci-contre, ci-dessus: *Le marché aux fleurs dans le centre ville; une bonne partie des habitants à Durban sont d'origine indienne.* Ci-contre, ci-dessous: *Le port de plaisance.*

Durban is South Africa's third largest city, its leading seaport and one of its most popular holiday destinations, numbering among its assets a splendid natural harbour, long and lovely beaches, and six glittering kilometres of seafront known as the 'Golden Mile'.

Durban ist die drittgrößte Stadt des Landes, sein führender Seehafen und wohl unbestreitbar der beliebteste Urlaubsort. Der vorzügliche, natürliche Hafen, die unendlichen, herrlichen Strände und die 6 km lange prächtige Strandpromenade, bekannt als 'Golden Mile', machen die Stadt besonders attraktiv.

Durban, la troisième ville d'Afrique du Sud, est la destination de vacances la plus prisée; son splendide port naturel, est le premier du pays. Durban a pour atout de longues étendues de très belles plages et six kilomètres de front de mer, le célèbre 'Golden Mile'.

Among the scenic delights of the fertile region between the KwaZulu-Natal Drakensberg and the Indian Ocean to the east are the Howick Falls (opposite), *a lovely cascade that plunges 95 m into the Mgeni River, and nearby Midmar dam and its nature reserve* (below). Left: *Zulu village women.*

Zu den landschaftlichen Genüßen der fruchtbaren Region zwischen den KwaZulu-Natal Drakensbergen und dem Indischen Ozean im Osten, zählen die Howick Fälle (gegenüber), *ein beeindruckender Wasserfall, der 95 m tief in den Mgenifluß stürzt, sowie der nahe Midmar Damm und Naturpark* (unten). Links: *Frauen in einem Zuludorf.*

Les chutes de Howick (ci-contre) *sont l'un des nombreux sites spectaculaires qu'offre cette région fertile, située entre le Drakensberg du KwaZulu-Natal et l'océan Indien à l'est. Une impressionnante cascade qui tombe 95 m plus bas dans la Mgeni River et, non loin de là, le barrage de Midmar et sa réserve* (ci-dessous). A gauche: *Des femmes zouloues.*

Between KwaZulu-Natal and the Eastern Cape is the Transkei region, traditional home to sections of the Xhosa people and a country of rivers, rolling green hills and a magnificent 280-km shoreline known as the Wild Coast. Above: *The remarkable 'Hole in the Wall' a detached cliff through which the sea thunders.* Opposite: *Village scene.* Left: *Xhosa women.*

Die Transkei liegt zwischen dem Ostkap und KwaZulu-Natal. Traditionelle Heimat vieler Xhosasippen, ist es ein Land von Flüßen, wogenden, grünen Hügeln und einer prachtvollen 280 km langen Küste, die Wilde Küste. Oben: *Das Meer braust durch das spektakuläre 'Loch in der Wand'.* Gegenüber: *Eine Dorfszene.* Links: *Typische Xhosafrauen.*

Le Transkei, situé entre le KwaZulu-Natal et l'est de la province du Cap, est traditionnellement le territoire d'une partie du peuple xhosa. C'est une région verdoyante et vallonnée aux nombreux cours d'eau et qui possède 280 km de côte splendide, appelée la Côte Sauvage. Ci-dessus: *L'extraordinaire 'Hole in the Wall' curiosité naturelle où vient s'engouffrer la mer.* Ci-contre: *Scène de village.* A gauche: *Des femmes Xhosas*

The famed Garden Route extends along the southern Cape shoreline from Storms River to Mossel Bay, the road running through an enchanting coastal terrace flanked by sea and mountain. Opposite, above: *The Storms River mouth.* Opposite, below: *The high bridge across the river's gorge.* Below: *The popular holiday resort of Plettenberg Bay.*

Von Storms River im südlichen Kap bis nach Mossel Bay, über Berge und durch Täler, durchquert die bekannte Garden Route eine reizvolle Küstenlandschaft. Gegenüber, oben: *Storms River, die Flußmündung.* Gegenüber, unten: *Die hohe Brücke über dem Flußtal.* Unten: *Plettenberg Bay, für viele Urlauber der schönste Ferienort.*

La célèbre Route des Jardins s'étend le long de la côte sud entre la Storms River et Mossel Bay. Elle longe une attrayante bande côtière que bordent la mer et la montagne. Ci-contre, ci-dessus: *L'embouchure de la Storms River.* Ci-contre, ci-dessous: *Le pont vertigineux qui enjambe la gorge.* Ci-dessous: *Plettenberg Bay, station balnéaire à la mode.*

Right: *The narrow sea entrance to Knysna's magnificent, 17-km-long lagoon is guarded by high sandstone cliffs known as The Heads. Linking Knysna with the attractive inland town of George is the 'Outeniqua Choo-tjoe'* (below), *a narrow-gauge, working steam-train.*

Rechts: *The Heads, hohe Sandsteinklippen, stehen Wache über der engen Meereseinfahrt in die prachtvolle 17-km-lange Lagune von Knysna. Die 'Outeniqua Choo-tjoe'* (unten) *Schmalspurbahn fährt regelmäßig zwischen Knysna und George.*

A droite: *L'étroite entrée du port–que gardent d'imposants promontoires de grès appelées Les Heads –qui s'ouvre sur le magnifique lagon de Knysna mesurant 17 km de long. Le petit train à vapeur et à voie étroite, le 'Outeniqua Choo-tjoe'* (ci-dessous), *relie Knysna à George, jolie petite ville dans l'arrière-pays.*

Between the towns of Knysna and Wilderness are several large and lovely stretches of water that attract a magnificent array of waterfowl and other birds. This is South Africa's 'Lake District', of which the Touws River (above) *is an integral part.* Left: *The Knysna-Tsitsikamma area sustains the country's largest expanse of indigenous high forest; this Outeniqua yellowwood is known as the Big Tree.*

Wunderschöne Seen, ein Paradies für Wasservögel, liegen zwischen den Orten Knysna und Wilderness. Dies ist Südafrikas Seengebiet, zu dem auch Touws River (oben) *zählt.* Links: *Der höchste Waldbestand einheimischer Bäume ist im Tsitsikammawald bei Knysna zu finden; dieser Outeniqua Gelbholzbaum ist der sogenannte 'Big Tree'.*

Entre Knysna et Wilderness, de magnifiques et vastes plans d'eau attirent toutes sortes d'oiseaux aquatiques. Cet endroit est le 'Lake District' (région des lacs) de l'Afrique du Sud qu'alimente principalement la Touws River (ci-dessus), A gauche: *La région de Tsitsikamma, la plus grande zone de forêts indigènes dans le pays; on appelle ce podocarpus géant le 'Big Tree'.*

North of the Garden Route, between the coastal rampart and the high Swartberg range, is a dry but fertile region called the Little Karoo, famed for its labyrinthine Cango Cave complex (left) *and its ostrich farms* (above). *Beyond the Swartberg, on the edge of the Great Karoo, is the Valley of Desolation* (opposite), *a gigantic jumble of wind-eroded dolorite formations.*

Eingeengt vom Küstenstreifen und einem Höhenzug, dem Swartberg, liegt die Kleine Karoo. Es ist ein trockenes, doch fruchtbares Gebiet, bekannt für sein Höhlenlabyrinth Cango Caves (links) *und seine Vogelstraußfarmen* (oben). *Jenseits der Swartberge, am Rand der Großen Karoo, liegt das Valley of Desolation–das Tal der Trostlosigkeit–* (gegenüber), *ein gigantisches Wirrwarr von windabgetragenen Basaltformationen.*

Au nord de la Route des Jardins–située entre le rempart formé par la bande côtière et la chaîne du Swartberg–s'étend la région sèche mais fertile que l'on appelle le Petit Karoo, qui est réputée pour ses Grottes de Cango, extraordinaire labyrinthe (à gauche) *et pour ses fermes d'élevage d'autruches* (ci-dessus). *Au-delà du Swartberg, en bordure du Grand Karoo, s'étend la Vallée de la Désolation* (ci-contre), *gigantesque enchevêtrement de formations rocheuses érodées.*

Opposite, bottom: *South Africa's oldest city nestles beneath the hugely looming, distinctively flat-topped massif of Table Mountain, one of the world's most familiar landmarks.* Right: *Visitors ascend the heights by cable car.* Below: *On the summit.* Opposite, top: *Busy St George's Mall in central Cape Town.*

Gegenüber, unten: *Südafrikas älteste Stadt liegt im Schatten des mächtigen, sich auftürmenden Tafelberges. Unverkennbar ist sein flacher Gipfel, eins der bekanntesten Wahrzeichen der Welt.* Rechts: *Besucher erreichen den Gipfel mit der Seilbahn.* Unten: *Auf dem Gipfel.* Gegenüber, oben: *Die geschäftige St. George's Mall im Stadtzentrum.*

Ci-contre, ci-dessous: *La plus ancienne ville d'Afrique du Sud, nichée au pied de l'imposante Montagne de la Table que caractérise un sommet plat et qui est l'un des sites les plus connus du monde.* A droite: *Des visiteurs montent en téléphérique.* Ci-dessous: *Au sommet.* En face, ci-dessus: *St George's Mall, rue piétonnière animée dans le centre ville.*

Rivalling Table Mountain as Cape Town's premier attraction is the new and imaginative waterfront development, a kaleidoscope of dockside bistros and bars, speciality shops, markets and museums. Above: *Victoria Basin.* Opposite, top: *Two Oceans Aquarium.* Opposite, bottom: *The Amphitheatre.*

Das kürzlich sanierte Hafenviertel, ein Kaleidoskop von Bistros, Bars, Fachgeschäften, Märkten und Museen, rivalisiert mit dem Tafelberg als Touristenattraktion der Stadt. Oben: *Das Viktoriabecken.* Gegenüber, oben: *Two Oceans Aquarium.* Gegenüber, unten: *Das Amphitheater.*

Rivalisant avec la Montagne de la Table en tant que premier site touristique au Cap, le Waterfront est un complexe séduisant qui abrite des bistros, des boutiques, des marchés et des musées. Ci-dessus: *Le Victoria Basin.* Ci-contre, ci-dessus: *Two Oceans Aquarium.* Ci-contre, ci-dessous: *L'Amphithéâtre.*

FRESH FRIED
AGFA AMPHITHEATRE
WATERFRONT
Our Children's Day
SPEAK UP FOR THE CHILDREN

The Cape Peninsula's shoreline is a paradise for summer sunbathers. Opposite, above and below: *The wide, white beaches of Clifton on the western, or Atlantic, seaboard.* Above: *Fish Hoek's beaches, on the east coast, are lapped by the warmer waters of False Bay.*

Das Küstengebiet der Halbinsel ist ein Paradies für Sonnenanbeter. Gegenüber, oben und unten: *Die weiten, weißen Strände von Clifton, an der atlantischen Küste.* Oben: *Das wärmere Wasser der False Bay schlägt an den Strand von Fish Hoek, an der Ostküste.*

Le littoral de la Péninsule du Cap est idéal en été pour les amateurs de bains de mer. Ci-contre, ci-dessus et ci-dessous: *Les étendues de sable blanc à Clifton sur la côte ouest.* Ci-dessus: *La plage de Fish Hoek, sur la côte est, que baignent les eaux chaudes de la Fausse Baie.*

At the Peninsula's southern extremity is Cape Point (left, and below left), *a massive promontory and part of the Cape of Good Hope Nature Reserve. It is off this headland that sightings of* The Flying Dutchman, *the ghost-ship destined to sail the seas until Judgment Day, have been recorded.*

Am südlichsten Zipfel der Halbinsel liegt die Kapspitze (links, und unten links), *ein mächtiges Vorgebirge und zum Teil Naturpark Cape of Good Hope Nature Reserve. Von hier ist das Geisterschiff* Der Fliegende Holländer *gesichtet worden, verdammt zur ewigen Umschiffung des Kaps.*

A l'extrémité sud de la Péninsule, la Pointe du Cap (à gauche, et ci-dessous à gauche), *promontoire massif qui fait partie de la réserve du Cap de Bonne Espérance. C'est de ce promontoire que, dit-on, on a aperçu le Vaisseau Fantôme, navire maudit condamné à errer au large jusqu'au jugement dernier.*

Left: *The harbour at Hout Bay, one of the Peninsula's most charming coastal villages: it nestles in a wide green valley flanked by tree-mantled hillsides. From here the coastal road runs south to cut through the steep cliffs beneath Chapman's Peak* (above), *from which the splendid views of both bay and mountain are unforgettable.*

Links: *Der Hafen von Hout Bay, eins der hübschesten Küstendörfer. Es liegt in einem weiten, grünen Tal, umgeben von waldbedeckten Hängen. Von hier führt die Küstenstraße in südlicher Richtung und schneidet durch die steilen Klippen des Chapman Peak* (oben), *mit einer herrlichen Aussicht über die Bucht und den Berg.*

A gauche: *Hout Bay, blotti au creux d'une vallée verdoyante; c'est l'un des villages les plus charmants de la côte et le point de départ de la route de corniche de Chapman's Peak* (ci-dessus), *route vers le sud qui offre des vues saisissantes sur la montagne et sur la baie.*

Opposite: *Groot Constantia is one of four estates situated on the Peninsula's 'wine route'. The elegant homestead was originally the home of Simon van der Stel, the outstanding early Cape governor, who lived there until his death in 1712.* Below: *Nearby Kirstenbosch ranks among the world's leading botanical gardens.*

Gegenüber: *Groot Constantia ist eins der vier Güter auf der 'Weinroute' der Kaphalbinsel. Das elegante Gut gehörte einst dem vortrefflichen Gouverneur, Simon van der Stel, der hier bis zu seinem Tod im Jahr 1712 lebte.* Unten: *Kirstenbosch, nahebei, zählt zu den führenden botanischen Gärten der Welt.*

Ci-contre: *Groot Constantia, l'un des quatre domaines faisant partie de la 'route des vins' de la Péninsule. L'élégant manoir fut à l'origine la demeure de Simon van der Stel, le gouverneur du Cap du début de la colonie. Il y vécut jusqu'à sa mort en 1712.* Ci-dessous: *Kirstenbosch, l'un des jardins botaniques les plus célèbres au monde.*

The countryside to the north and east of Cape Town is an entrancing compound of mountains and fertile valleys, historic towns and gracious Cape Dutch manor-houses, vineyards and orchards heavy with fruit. Below: *A corner of Stellenbosch, which was founded in 1679.* Right: *Wine-tasting at Nederburg.* Opposite: *The beautiful Franschhoek valley.*

Die Landschaft nördlich und östlich von Kapstadt ist eine hinreißende Mischung von Bergen und fruchtbaren Tälern, historischen Städten und graziösen 'Cape Dutch' Wohnhäusern, frucht-beladenen Wein- und Obstgärten. Unten: *Ein Teil von Stellenbosch, 1679 gegründet.* Rechts: *Weinprobe auf Nederburg.* Gegenüber: *Das liebliche Tal von Franschhoek .*

L'arrière-pays situé au nord et à l'est du Cap est enchanteur: c'est une succession harmonieuse de hautes montagnes et de vallées fertiles, de villes anciennes aux élégantes demeures de style hollandais du Cap, de beaux vignobles et de riches vergers. Ci-dessous: *Un quartier de Stellenbosch, fondée en 1679.* A droite: *Dégustation de vins à Nederburg.* Ci-contre: *La ravissante vallée de Franschhoek.*

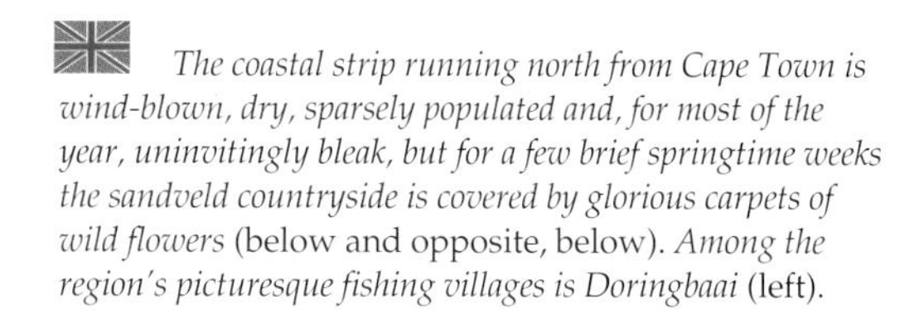

The coastal strip running north from Cape Town is wind-blown, dry, sparsely populated and, for most of the year, uninvitingly bleak, but for a few brief springtime weeks the sandveld countryside is covered by glorious carpets of wild flowers (below and opposite, below). *Among the region's picturesque fishing villages is Doringbaai* (left).

Der Küstenstreifen nördlich von Kapstadt is wind-verweht, trocken, spärlich besiedelt und bietet fast das ganze Jahr hindurch einen trostlosen Anblick, außer im Frühling, wenn sich strahlende Blumenteppiche (unten und gegenüber, unten) *ausbreiten. Doringbaai* (links) *ist eins der malerischsten Fischerdörfer in der Gegend.*

La bande côtière, qui s'étend au nord du Cap, est battue par les vents, aride et peu peuplée. C'est la plupart de l'année un lieu inhospitalier, à l'exception du printemps lorsque, pendant quelques semaines à peine, le sol sablonneux se couvre d'un tapis multicolore de fleurs sauvages (ci-dessous et ci-contre, ci-dessous). *Doringbaai* (à gauche) *est l'un des petits ports de pêche pittoresques de la région.*

Among the attractive little seaside villages to the east of Cape Town is Waenhuiskrans, also known as Arniston (left), *notable for its fine hotel and its charming old fisherman's cottages.* Below: *The lighthouse at Cape Agulhas, the most southerly point of the African continent.*

Waenhuiskrans, auch bekannt als Arniston (links), *mit seinem erstklassigen Hotel und reizvollen alten Fischerhütten, ist eins der schönsten Küstendörfer östlich von Kapstadt.* Unten: *Der Leuchtturm am Kap Agulhas, südlichster Punkt in Afrika.*

Situé à l'est du Cap, Waenhuiskrans, aussi appelé Arniston, est un joli village connu pour son bel hôtel et ses pittoresques petites maisons de pêcheurs. Ci-dessous: *Le phare du Cap des Aiguilles, à l'extrémité sud du continent africain.*

Struik Publishers
(a division of New Holland Publishing (South Africa) (Pty) Ltd), 80 McKenzie Street Cape Town 8001, South Africa

New Holland Publishing is a member of the Johnnic Publishing Group
Website: ***www.struik.co.za***

First published 1993
8 10 9 7

Anthony Bannister *p 17 (top);* **Leo Braak** *p 18 (bottom);* **Gerald Cubitt** *front and back cover, pp 44/45;* **Roger de la Harpe** *front cover (inset, bottom) [ABPL], p 20 (bottom) [Natal Parks Board];* **Richard du Toit** *p 19 (top) [ABPL];* **Clem Haagner** *p 46 (bottom) [ABPL];* **John Haigh** *p 1;* **Lex Hes** *p 16, p 17 (bottom);* **Carol Hughes** *p 14 (top) [ABPL];* **Walter Knirr** *front cover (inset, top), p 3, p 4 (bottom), p 5 (top and bottom), pp 6/7, p 8 (top), pp 10/11, pp 12/13, p 14 (bottom), p 18 (top), p 20 (top and centre), p 21, pp 22/23, pp 24/25, p 26 (bottom), p 27, pp 28/29, p 30, p 31 (top), pp 32/33, p 35 (bottom), pp 36/37, pp 38/39, p 40 (bottom), p 41 (top), pp 42/43, p 46 (top), p 47, p 48;* **Tim Liversedge** *p 15 [ABPL];* **Londolozi Marketing** *p 19 (bottom);* **Herman Potgieter** *p 9 (left and right);* **Struik Image Library** *p 34, p 35 (top), p 40 (top), p 41 (bottom);* **Studio Jano** *p 8 (bottom);* **Mark van Aardt** *p 4 (top), p 26 (top), p 31 (bottom).*
ABPL = Anthony Bannister Photo Library

French translation by Cécile Spottiswoode
German translation by Ursula Stevens
Designed by Alix Gracie
Typesetting by Struik DTP, Cape Town
Reproduction by Unifoto (Pty) Ltd, Cape Town
Printed and bound by Kyodo Printing Co (Singapore) Pte Ltd

ISBN 1 86825 435 6